PEACHTREE

THE UNIVERSE
SPACE EXPLORATION

ABDO
Publishing Company

A Buddy Book **by Marcia Zappa**

Buddy BOOKS
The Universe

VISIT US AT
www.abdopublishing.com

Published by ABDO Publishing Company, 8000 West 78th Street, Edina, Minnesota 55439.

Printed in the United States of America, North Mankato, Minnesota.
102010
012011

♻ PRINTED ON RECYCLED PAPER

Coordinating Series Editor: Rochelle Baltzer
Contributing Editors: Megan M. Gunderson, BreAnn Rumsch, Sarah Tieck
Graphic Design: Maria Hosley
Cover Photograph: *NASA*.
Interior Photographs/Illustrations: *AP Photo*: AP Photo (p. 12), Courtesy of Earth Sciences and Image Analysis Laboratory, NASA Johnson Space Center (p. 29), NASA (p. 24), Pat Sullivan (p. 25), TASS (p. 7); *NASA*: ESA and M. Livio and the Hubble Heritage Team (STScl/AURA) (p. 5), Sandra Joseph, Tony Gray, Robert Murray, Mike Kerley May 31, 2008 (p. 17), JPL (p. 9), JPL-Caltech/University Arizona/Texas A&M University (p. 11), MSFC (p. 7), NASA (pp. 8, 13, 17, 19, 21, 23, 27, 28, 30), National Space Science Data Center (p. 28); *Photo Researchers, Inc.*: NASA (p. 15).

Library of Congress Cataloging-in-Publication Data

Zappa, Marcia, 1985-
  Space exploration / Marcia Zappa.
    p. cm. -- (The universe)
  ISBN 978-1-61714-692-3
  1. Astronautics--Juvenile literature. 2. Outer space--Exploration--Juvenile literature. I. Title.
TL793.Z294 2011
  629.4'1--dc22
                                      2010032597

Table Of Contents

Exploring Space

People have observed objects in the night sky for thousands of years. At first, they could only study space objects from the ground.

Over time, people dreamed of sending spacecraft into space. In 1957, this dream came true. The age of space **exploration** began.

Space is full of interesting objects
such as galaxies, stars, and planets.

The Space Race

Many countries wanted to reach space first. The United States and the Soviet Union tried very hard to be first. This became known as the space race.

In 1957, the Soviet Union **launched** the first spacecraft into space. A few months later, the United States followed. In 1958, a group formed to direct U.S. space **exploration**. It was called **NASA**.

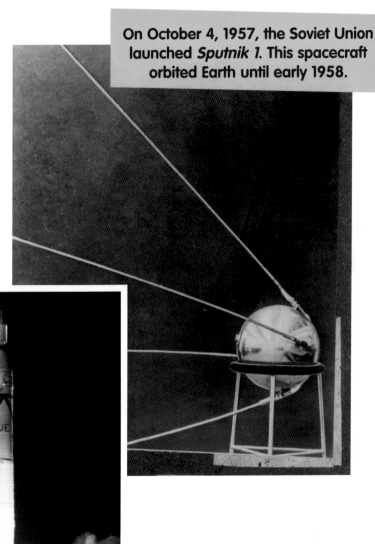

On October 4, 1957, the Soviet Union launched *Sputnik 1*. This spacecraft orbited Earth until early 1958.

The United States worked hard to match the success of *Sputnik 1*. It launched *Explorer 1* on January 31, 1958.

Probing the Universe

The first spacecraft were space probes. Rockets **launch** them into space. Space probes fly without a pilot. They carry cameras and other tools that collect data and send it to Earth.

Long ago, very little was known about how space would affect astronauts. This made probes a safer option for early exploration.

Probes that orbit a planet, a moon, or another space object are called artificial satellites.

Some probes land on or **orbit** space objects. Others follow paths through space. Many probes do not return from their **missions**. But some collect samples to bring back to Earth!

Space probes can travel farther than spacecraft with **astronauts**. In 1965, **NASA** began sending probes to study the sun. And in 1976, two probes landed on Mars!

In recent years, probes have visited faraway planets. These include Jupiter, Saturn, Uranus, and Neptune.

A probe called *Phoenix* was sent to Mars in 2007. It found ice below the planet's surface!

11

Visiting Space

Soon after the first space probe flight, scientists worked to send people into space. In 1961, Soviet Yuri Gagarin became the first **astronaut** in space. Over the next few years, others followed.

Yuri Gagarin orbited Earth one time. His flight lasted 108 minutes.

Before long, scientists began planning a trip to the moon. On July 20, 1969, U.S. **astronauts** Neil Armstrong and Buzz Aldrin walked on the moon. They were the first to ever do this!

U.S. astronauts landed on the moon six times between 1969 and 1972. They brought back samples of soil and rocks. And, they set up science tools.

Early **astronauts** traveled in space capsules. Capsules were made to be used only once.

Rockets **launched** space capsules. Then, they separated from them. Many rockets fell back toward Earth. Others flew off into space.

After completing their **missions**, space capsules returned to Earth. They used large sails called parachutes to slow down their fall.

Most space capsules were made to land in the ocean. The water made a softer surface for the crash.

There and Back Again

Around the 1970s, scientists created a new spacecraft to carry **astronauts**. It was called a space shuttle.

Space shuttles still used rockets to **launch**. But, they had wings and could land like an airplane. This made them reusable. In 1981, the United States launched the first space shuttle, *Columbia*.

Space shuttles were built to make up to 100 flights!

Space shuttle **missions** last 5 to 16 days. Inside a space shuttle, **astronauts** ride in a cabin. They observe space objects and do science experiments. Space shuttles also carry probes into space.

One important job of space shuttle astronauts is fixing satellites.

Living in Space

Space stations are another type of spacecraft. **Astronauts** can live and work in them for long periods of time.

Space stations **orbit** Earth. They are used to observe space and do science experiments. Space stations also store tools and **fuel**.

Parts of large space stations are launched into space
on rockets. Then, astronauts put them together.

In 1971, the Soviet Union sent the first space station into space. It was called Salyut 1. In 1973, the United States **launched** its first space station, Skylab.

In 1998, scientists started building the International Space Station (ISS). The first three **astronauts** moved into this large station in 2000. Today, six crew members at a time live there.

The ISS is a group project among more than 15 countries.

Spacecraft such as shuttles bring astronauts to and from the ISS.

Space Travel

Astronauts face different conditions in space than on Earth. The force of gravity is less noticeable in a moving spacecraft. This makes astronauts float around as if they are weightless!

Some astronauts sleep strapped to a surface similar to a bed and a pillow. Others sleep floating in the air!

Objects in space can get very hot or very cold. So, a spacecraft has a system that keeps the temperature at the right level.

There is almost no air in space. So, spacecraft store air in tanks. Fans send fresh air to the crew. And, filters capture used air.

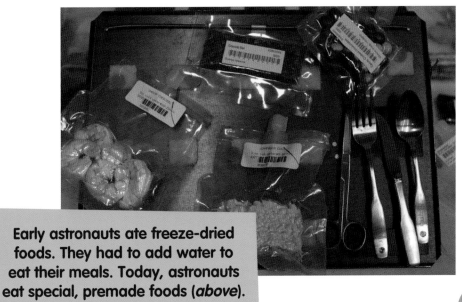

Early astronauts ate freeze-dried foods. They had to add water to eat their meals. Today, astronauts eat special, premade foods (*above*).

Outside the spacecraft, **astronauts** wear special suits. These suits **protect** them from heat and cold. They also guard astronauts from being hit by small space objects.

Space suits have everything needed to survive in space for about seven hours. This includes air, water, and tools to remove waste.

Gloves are an important part of a space suit.
They are strong to protect an astronaut's hands.
But, they are also thin so the astronaut can work.

Fact Trek

In 1959, the space probe *Luna 3* took pictures of the far side of the moon. It had never been seen before!

Space probes bring supplies to space stations. These include water, food, and mail.

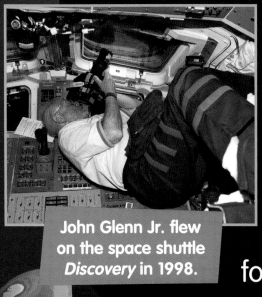

John Glenn Jr. flew on the space shuttle _Discovery_ in 1998.

The oldest **astronaut** to travel to space is American John Glenn Jr. He was 77 years old when he went to space for the second time!

From 1994 to 1995, Russian astronaut Valery Polyakov was in space for almost 438 days in a row! This is the longest space trip anyone has taken.

Voyage to Tomorrow

People continue to **explore** space. The U.S. space shuttle program ended in 2010. Scientists are working on a new type of spacecraft. It is named *Orion*.

Scientists plan to use *Orion* to carry astronauts to the moon and to Mars!

Important Words

astronaut a person who is trained for space travel.

explore to go into in order to make a discovery or to have an adventure. Exploration is the act of exploring.

fuel (FYOOL) something burned to give heat or power.

gravity a natural force that pulls toward the center of a space object. It also pulls space objects toward each other.

launch to send off with force.

mission the sending of spacecraft to do certain jobs.

NASA National Aeronautics Space Administration. NASA is run by the U.S. government to study Earth, our solar system, and outer space.

orbit to follow a path around a space object.

protect (pruh-TEHKT) to guard against harm or danger.

Web Sites

To learn more about **space exploration**, visit ABDO Publishing Company online. Web sites about **space exploration** are featured on our Book Links page. These links are routinely monitored and updated to provide the most current information available.

www.abdopublishing.com

INDEX